ZOE SALDANA

Acting with Heart and Heroism

Jean D. Stafford

Copyright @ 2024 By Jean D. Stafford

All rights reserved. No part of this book may be reproduced, distributed, or transmitted in any form or by any means, including photocopying, recording, or other electronic or mechanical methods, without the prior written permission of the publisher, except in the case of brief quotations embodied in critical reviews and specific other noncommercial uses permitted by copyright law.

Table of contents

Introduction: Lights, Camera, Action!

Chapter 1: A Girl with Big Dreams

Chapter 2: The Early Days of Acting

Chapter 3: Stepping into the Spotlight

Chapter 4: Becoming a Sci-Fi Superstar

Chapter 5: More Than Just a Star

Chapter 6: Strong Women in Movies

Chapter 7: A Heart for Change

Chapter 8: Learning from Challenges

Chapter 9: The Power of Being Yourself

Chapter 10: Family and Friendship

Fun facts about Zoe Saldana

Conclusion: Reaching for your stars

Introduction: Lights, Camera, Action!

Film is a beautiful place of imagination, adventure, and limitless possibilities. We can go into space, delve into the ocean's depths, and discover other worlds without ever getting up from our chairs. Those who shine so brightly that they become more significant than life and inspire millions of people worldwide are the stars at the center of this world. One of such celebrities is Zoe Saldana. Her path to success, however, was challenging; it was paved with aspirations, arduous labor, and innumerable hours of commitment.

On June 19, 1978, Zoe was born into a loving and vibrant family in the bustling city of Passaic, New Jersey. Zoe has a remarkable passion for the arts from a young age. Like many kids, she was amazed by the world around her, but her true passion was acting and dancing. For Zoe, dance, in particular, became a means of self-expression. It was more than simply moving her body to music; it was a language unto itself, a means of communicating with the heart and telling stories without words. However, Zoe's love of dancing was broader than just a single style. Her insatiable curiosity and willingness to try new things pushed her to pursue acting.

Zoe faced difficulties along the way. Growing up wasn't always simple, in actuality. Both of Zoe's parents are initially from the Dominican Republic, and they both hailed from low-income families. Living in New Jersey also presented its own set of challenges. Zoe's life would be significantly impacted by the death of her father when she was just nine years old. No kid should have to go through the grief of losing a parent at such a young age, but Zoe displayed exceptional fortitude under those trying circumstances. She relied on her family, particularly her mother, who put much effort into keeping everything together. Zoe's love for her family did not waver in the face of adversity, and her will to succeed grew stronger. She learned the importance of resiliency and tenacity from these experiences, which would later aid her in navigating the acting industry.

Even though many children aspire to be famous, Zoe's goals are always more significant. The idea of telling stories, taking on the role of a character, and putting herself in other people's shoes to depict the world from their perspective drew her to the spotlight, not just the attention. She cherished the potency of narrative. She loved that performing might move people's emotions and elicit laughter, tears, and even thought. As Zoe became older, it became evident that acting was her vocation rather than only a pastime. But it was more complex than it would seem to become a Hollywood celebrity.

Zoe had to learn how to deal with rejection early on because auditions were brutal in the acting industry. Before receiving her first significant break, she encountered many "no's." But she persisted because she understood that every tryout, even the ones that didn't lead to a part, was a step closer to her goal. Zoe finally got her first significant role in the 2000 film Center

Stage, which was about a group of ballet dancers after years of training, auditioning, and learning the skill of acting. Her journey began with this role, demonstrating the power that may arise when opportunity and hard effort collide. Additionally, it showed to the globe that Zoe was a rising star.

However, her passion, tenacity, and skill set her apart. Zoe knew that to succeed in the business, she would need to be more than just a skilled actor; she would also need to be prepared to battle for the parts she desired, persevere through difficulties, and never stop honing her craft. From portraying a strong soldier in **Star Trek** to a fierce warrior in **Avatar**, she kept playing various roles. In both films, Zoe demonstrated to the public that women could be just as courageous, strong, and brave as men. She didn't merely do parts; she became the characters and gave them life in a way that inspired viewers to believe in them.

In 2014, Zoe played Gamora in **Guardians of the Galaxy**, one of her most well-known performances. In her portrayal as the green-skinned warrior, Zoe demonstrated her ability to play a character with heart, nuance, and complexity and handle action-packed superhero roles. Zoe's portrayal of Gamora moved fans worldwide because she was more than a fierce fighter; she had a background full of suffering and sorrow. Zoe's reputation as one of Hollywood's most gifted and well-respected actors was cemented by this role.

Zoe was an inspiration not only because of her work on-screen but also because of her work off-screen. In addition to being a wife and mother, Zoe is also a philanthropist and an advocate for topics that are important to her. Zoe has always prioritized her family over her hectic profession. She has frequently expressed how much she values her kids and her desire to set an example for them. She has also used her position to promote causes such as women's rights, environmental preservation, and the value of representation in Hollywood. As much as Zoe is passionate about performing, she is equally committed to improving the world.

Through her work, Zoe has demonstrated to the world that pursuing your goals alone is insufficient; you also need to give back, stand up for what's right, and use your voice to change the world. She has demonstrated that being a real hero can sometimes involve utilizing your heart, talent, and strength to improve the world rather than donning a cape or engaging in combat with extraterrestrials. She inspires others, perseveres through challenges, and never gives up on the idea that everything is possible.

You are cordially invited to accompany Zoe on her amazing adventure through this book. It's a path full of hardships and victories, happiness and sorrow, and discovering what it means to be genuinely brilliant. It tells the tale of a girl who took a dream and made it into something far more significant than she ever could have anticipated. Zoe's journey from her initial foray into the acting industry to becoming one of the most important actors of her time is evidence that everything is achievable with a lot of heart, a little magic, and a lot of hard work.

Chapter 1: A Girl with Big Dreams

Zoe Saldana was merely a little girl in New Jersey with lofty aspirations long before she was starring in films like **Avatar** and **Guardians of the Galaxy** before her name became a representation of bravery and fortitude. Zoe grew up in the vibrant town of Passaic, surrounded by culture, love, and the rhythms of daily life. Her father, Aridio, and mother, Asalia, hail from the Dominican Republic, and they infused their family with the warmth of their culture. In addition to the typical sounds of daily living, Zoe's home was where dancing, laughter, and music were as ubiquitous as breathing.

She was constantly eager to learn new things and was captivated by the world around her. She quickly developed a passion for movement. Dance became Zoe's first love, and she was constantly on the go, whether dancing in her living room or on the pavement outdoors.

She felt more alive with each beat of the music, which seemed to speak straight to her soul. For Zoe, dance was a means of communication with the outside world, not just a pastime. She understood that dancing was where she felt most at home but could not articulate her joy there.

Zoe was drawn to dancing because of the storytelling element as much as the excitement of movement. She could convey feelings and tales that words could not adequately describe with each spin, leap, and elegant leap. For Zoe, dance was an unwritten language that allowed her to connect with the world. Dancing made her feel like she belonged, whether practicing alone or performing with friends. She felt strong, self-assured, and capable of anything as a result. She had no idea that her passion for using dance to express herself would serve as the basis for her career in acting, where she would specialize in performing stories.

Despite Zoe's passion for dancing, she didn't have a direct path to Hollywood. It was replete with detours and uneasy moments. However, one thing remained constant: Zoe was adamant. Even if it meant venturing outside her comfort zone, she was adamant about pursuing her dreams. Zoe was pushing herself to become more than just a dancer by the time she was a teenager. She soon began to dream of becoming more than a dancer after realizing that her passion for performance could translate into the acting industry. She wanted to be an actress who could play any part, no matter how big or small.

Zoe's passion for theater served as the foundation for her acting career. Zoe was fascinated by the world of theater and performance when many children her age were preoccupied with sports, computer games, or school. To hone her skills, she started trying out for local theatrical performances. She had previously learned discipline, expression, and the value of working hard to reach your goals from her love of dance, and she was now transferring these principles to her acting career. But Zoe had to face rejection, just like many other young idealists. It was more complicated. At times, it looked as though the ideal she had worked so hard to achieve might not materialize, and not every audition resulted in a role.

However, Zoe's fortitude was evident. She learned from each rejection rather than allowing it to break her. Every "no" she received simply strengthened her resolve to improve, put in more effort, and remain even more dedicated to her goals. During this initial phase of hardship and perseverance, Zoe started to recognize a significant aspect of herself: she wasn't merely gifted; she was prepared to put in the effort to achieve her goals. She refused to accept things as given to her. She desired to demonstrate to the world that she had the grit, talent, and compassion necessary for success. She would use this attitude and her will to persevere throughout her career to help her deal with the highs and lows of the entertainment business.

She found support in her family as well. In particular, her mother was crucial in helping Zoe pursue her goals. Her mother reminded her that anything was achievable if she put in the necessary effort and had faith in herself, even during difficult times. Zoe learned the value of self-respect and remaining loyal to oneself from her powerful mother. These principles formed Zoe's cornerstone and would serve as her compass throughout her life, directing her not only in her professional engagements but also in her personal choices and interactions.

Zoe had already established herself in the theater industry by the time she was 17. She relocated to New York City, which presented both chances and difficulties. Zoe was prepared to overcome any challenge because her goal was to become an actress. She was aware that she would be able to put herself to the ultimate test in New York City with its never-ending theater performances and auditions. And she put herself to the test. She kept going to acting classes and tried out for one role after another, and gradually, her goal of becoming an actor began to take shape.

But Zoe was more than just an actress. She never lost sight of her first love while she refined her skills and became a better dancer. She was able to depict characters with nuance and accuracy thanks to her dancing training's fluidity, grace, and discipline. She always brought the same passion and enthusiasm to her on-screen performances as she had to her dance routines.

Zoe's possibilities increased along with her talent. Her passion for acting, love of dancing, and commitment to her goals started showing in everything she did. Every performance gave her the chance to show off her heart as well as her talent. Beginning in her living room and continuing throughout her adolescence, Zoe's passion for storytelling would soon propel her to success. As she practiced for a show or waited through auditions, she was unaware she was about to experience something monumental. She had no idea that she would soon be appearing in some of the biggest films in the world in addition to local theaters. One thing was sure, though: Zoe would give it her all no matter where her aspirations led her.

Her adventure officially began at that point. Zoe Saldana was just starting her journey to prominence, having gone from a young kid in New Jersey who loved dancing to a resolute actress desperate for opportunities. Her love for dance and the lessons she learned from it shaped how she approached everything—her work ethic, character, and drive to succeed.

Chapter 2: The Early Days of Acting

Because of her passion for dancing, Zoe Saldana was introduced to the world of performing, but she soon realized that acting was her true calling. Even though Zoe was enthralled with the beauty of dance and movement, there was something unique about taking the stage in front of a crowd that ignited a different type of magic for her. She found that acting allowed her to bring stories to life, change into other characters, and connect with people in ways that were impossible with just words and dance.

Zoe's initial forays into performing were both glamorous and straightforward. Like many aspiring actresses, she had to deal with rejection and uncertainty until she found her footing. In New Jersey, where little parts and performances may provide an actor with the ideal amount of exposure, she started by trying out for local theater plays. These initial auditions were exciting as well as nerve-racking. Zoe was bringing a character to life for an audience and engaging them in a manner that only an actor could, so she wasn't just performing for herself. The stage became a place where Zoe could challenge herself to be someone else, express herself fully, and experience the power of narrative.

Acting, Zoe soon discovered, was more than simply hitting marks and memorizing lines. It was about comprehending the reasons, emotions, and thoughts of the character she was portraying. She aspired to embody the character rather than only play it. For Zoe, performing was a means of self-discovery, a chance to put herself in other people's shoes and see their world. Zoe gave her everything to her parts, whether as a courageous soldier, a romantic heroine, or a troubled adolescent. Her characters were influenced by her personal experiences and her observations of the behavior of others around her.

When Zoe relocated to New York City, the center of American theater and performance, at 17, her goal made a significant leap forward. Opportunities abound in the city, but it's also daunting. Zoe was determined to take on the task because she had witnessed her mother struggle for years to earn a living and provide for their family. She kept trying out, frequently getting turned down one after the other, but her spirit remained unflinching. No matter how many doors were shut in her face, she understood that the only way to recover was to keep moving forward. Zoe's real acting career started to take form in New York.

Her first significant break occurred when she was cast in a production of the city's popular musical, **Joseph and the Amazing Technicolor Dreamcoat**. Zoe poured herself into the part, bringing to each performance her passion for dancing and her developing acting skills. She gained notoriety for her commitment, zeal, and enthusiasm on stage. She had a natural gift that enthralled spectators, and her performances were electric—full of passion and intensity. Zoe did more than deliver words and hit her targets; she evoked an emotion in the audience. She convinced them that the role she was portraying was fundamental.

Early theater experiences taught Zoe some of the most valuable things that would serve her well throughout her career, including the value of commitment, self-control, and the persuasiveness of narrative. Every performance at the theater offered an opportunity to develop, evolve, and try new things. Zoe liked acting as she grew more at ease on stage. She could fully express the suppressed emotions and let them run wild on stage, where she could be herself. It was a location where she could meet people and, more significantly, push herself to become an artist rather than merely a performer.

However, Zoe started to develop as an actor outside of theater. Knowing this was where she could make a difference, she immediately focused on the film and television industries. She sought every chance to get into Hollywood and tried out for TV series, short films, and advertisements. She had the same difficulties as many would-be actors: protracted waiting lists, unsuccessful auditions, and periods of uncertainty. But Zoe's unwavering faith in her capacity for success kept her going. She was aware that she was destined to be an actress.

Her perseverance paid off in 2000, as she was cast in **Center Stage**, her first significant motion picture role. Zoe played a dancer in this film who learns to express herself through dance while juggling the pressures of her career. The movie constituted a significant turning point in Zoe's career by allowing her to merge her love of dancing with her recently discovered passion for acting. Despite not being a big box office success, the movie was praised by critics, and Zoe's performance was particularly noteworthy. She demonstrated that she was a skilled dancer and a multifaceted actress with a genuine gift for giving characters life. Zoe established herself in Hollywood, showing she was more than prepared for the big stage.

Zoe took on various responsibilities as her career developed, each becoming increasingly difficult and unique. She didn't want to be classified as a particular kind of character. She wished to demonstrate her versatility as an actor to the world. Zoe always gave it her all, whether she was portraying an emotionally complex character in **The Words**, a strong, courageous leader in **wf3#_#by of the Galaxy**, or a futuristic warrior in **Avatar**. She gave every role her all, utilizing her theater skills to give her characters nuance and realism. She was living and breathing every second, every sentence, every gesture, not just playing a character on film.

Despite the success of her cinematic career, Zoe never lost her passion for the stage. She had learned how to connect with an audience, be in the present, and deliver a tale in a way that felt authentic on stage. She always remembered the passion that began it all and brought these lessons into every film. Zoe's acting was more than just her; she firmly believed in the value of teamwork and the enchantment of working with a group of gifted people to create something truly unique. Zoe knew she had discovered her genuine passion the moment she took the stage for her first performance. Acting was a way of life, not just a career. She could be herself there and yet transform into someone else entirely; she could make people think, laugh, and cry. Zoe had discovered her home in a world where stories came to life.

Chapter 3: Stepping into the Spotlight

Her early film performances helped to shape Zoe Saldana's career, establish her as a bright talent, and ultimately make her one of Hollywood's most famous actors. Her path to stardom wasn't an overnight triumph. Her move from theater to film was characterized by several calculated decisions, a commitment to her art, and a readiness to accept challenging and varied roles. She was able to establish a solid career foundation, show her dedication, and display her adaptability in these early jobs.

In 2000, Zoe landed her first significant film role in the drama **Center Stage**, which followed a group of budding ballet dancers. Zoe's performance in this movie was notable because of her innate charm and dance experience, even though her character, Eva, wasn't the main character. She demonstrated her acting and dancing skills in **Center Stage** by portraying a passionate and nuanced dancer. It was a significant turning point in her career since it allowed her to collaborate with gifted performers and get in front of moviegoers. The movie was well-received by youthful viewers and dance fans, which helped Zoe become well-known early on and start to build her career.

However, Zoe's major Hollywood break came from her part in the 2003 movie **Pirates of the Caribbean: The Curse of the Black Pearl**. Zoe entered a franchise that would become a worldwide phenomenon by portraying Anamaria, a pirate with a fiery attitude. This part marked a sea change for Zoe because it demonstrated her ability to compete with an ensemble cast that included Keira Knightley, Orlando Bloom, and Johnny Depp. Even though Anamaria wasn't the main character, Zoe's standout performance demonstrated her keen comedic timing, physicality, and capacity to impact each scene. She gained international recognition and credibility as a serious actor in an action-packed blockbuster by appearing in such a well-liked movie, which led to other possibilities in high-profile productions.

In 2004, Zoe landed her next significant part in Steven Spielberg's **The Terminal**. Although Zoe's role in this movie was smaller than Tom Hanks' lead, she portrayed a flight attendant named Dolores, further enhancing her already rising popularity. Zoe gained significant experience on a big motion picture set by working with one of Hollywood's most renowned directors, Spielberg. She gained knowledge of the intricacies of working on a large production, including how to balance her performance with that of seasoned performers and comprehend the technical aspects of filmmaking. As Zoe became more well-known for her ability to fit in with more significant, more intricate movie projects, being a part of such a prominent project helped cement her position in Hollywood.

That same year, she co-starred with Ashton Kutcher and Bernie Mac in the comedy **Guess Who**. In this film, Zoe portrayed Theresa, a man's fiancée who introduces his new companion to his parents. Since she was now working in comedy, a whole other genre, the job allowed her to demonstrate her versatility further. Zoe's ability to give more than simply intense or muscular performances was presented to Hollywood by this contrast with her prior dramatic or action roles. Casting directors began to notice her versatility and range as a bright talent because of her ability to transition between genres and yet give powerful performances.

But Zoe's breakthrough performance in 2009 as Neytiri in **Avatar** was what made her a household name. Despite being several years away, this movie resulted from Zoe's hard work in her early career. She had been prepared for a role of this size by every audition, every tiny role, and every chance to collaborate with brilliant directors. However, Zoe had established a reputation as a varied actress before **Avatar** thanks to her early work in comedies, dramas, and action movies. Zoe was prepared to portray a nuanced, sensitive character in a ground-breaking film on the verge of becoming a cultural sensation when James Cameron cast her as Neytiri.

Through her early film appearances, Zoe gained insight into what it required to succeed in Hollywood, including how to reconcile contributing as an individual performer with being a team member. They taught her how to perform well under pressure, deal with the challenges of playing a female lead in action and adventure genres that men dominate, and remain professional while pushing the limits of her acting skills. No matter how big or small, every movie allowed Zoe to improve her abilities, boost her self-esteem, and establish a strong career in the motion picture business.

By the time Avatar was released, Zoe had already demonstrated her ability to succeed in small, character-driven movies and large blockbuster franchises. She was a popular choice for essential roles in Hollywood because of her ability to easily switch across genres and give standout performances in various movies. In the early years of her career, she prepared for her eventual ascent to fame by taking on a variety of parts that challenged her skills and taught her the ins and outs of the film business.

With significant parts in high-profile franchises like **Guardians of the Galaxy** and smaller, independent films that demonstrated her range as an actor, Zoe solidified her reputation in the following years. As her career progressed, Zoe showed that she was an actor with longevity rather than merely a fad. She established a reputation in Hollywood that would soon be associated with strength, adaptability, and remarkable performances thanks to her early parts in **Center Stage**, **Pirates of the Caribbean**, and other films.

Chapter 4: Becoming a Sci-Fi Superstar

When Zoe Saldana landed two famous parts that would define her career and forever alter how people viewed her as an actress—Neytiri in **Avatar** and **Guardians of the Galaxy***1—her Hollywood career reached its pinnacle. Zoe brought these tough, strong, and independent female characters to life with such realism, depth, and passion that they won over fans worldwide. In addition to showcasing Zoe's extraordinary skill, these parts allowed her to portray strong, multifaceted characters that audiences found incredibly compelling.

She played Neytiri, a Na'vi princess and accomplished warrior from the extraterrestrial continent of Pandora, in James Cameron's 2009 film **Avatar**. One character who epitomizes grit, tenacity, and wisdom is Neytiri. She is a mighty warrior protecting her civilization from human intruders threatening her homeland. Zoe's portrayal of

Neytiri is captivating from the moment we see her in the movie. She embraces the role's physicality to the fullest, which was difficult given the heavy reliance on motion capture technology to portray a blue-skinned, 10-foot-tall alien with unearthly powers.

Zoe's portrayal in **Avatar** went beyond the role's physical requirements. Her portrayal of Neytiri's depth of emotion made the character memorable. Neytiri is a character who is passionate, kind, and loving, in addition to being a warrior. Zoe successfully conveyed this complexity in her portrayal of a lady divided between her obligation to her people and her developing bond with the human protagonist Jake Sully (Sam Worthington). Zoe exhibits a broad spectrum of emotions in her role as Neytiri, including intense devotion, profound grief, and emotional resolve. She created Neytiri, one of the most recognizable characters in science fiction movies, by portraying the fragility of her romance with Jake and her intense devotion to her people. Zoe was more than just your average action hero because of her nuanced acting, which gave the character depth.

Neytiri possesses not only physical strength but also mental and emotional fortitude. Neytiri's steadfast adherence to her principles and dedication to her people make her one of Hollywood's most captivating female characters in a world of strife, devastation, and unfamiliarity. Zoe's skill as an actor is demonstrated by her ability to highlight the value of these attributes even in the sweeping spectacle of **Avatar**. Viewers viewed her as a hero because of her fearless portrayal of Neytiri, and her courage, power, and wisdom inspired both men and women.

In the 2014 film **Guardians of the Galaxy**, Zoe played Gamora, another tough, strong, and multifaceted character. Thanos, the evil warlord in the Marvel Cinematic Universe, adopted Gamora as his daughter. She was brought up to be an assassin and is torn over her history and her part in Thanos' devastation. Zoe portrays Gamora in a complex way full of fury, tenderness, and a desire for atonement. Although Gamora is fundamentally a fighter, she bears the emotional burden of her previous deeds and her battle to escape Thanos' rule.

Every battle that Gamora engages in demonstrates her ferocity, and Zoe's dedication to making this character come to life is evident in her fighting prowess and physicality. However, what makes Zoe one of the most notable characters in **Guardians of the Galaxy** is the depth of feeling she infuses Gamora with. Gamora is more than just a heartless, cunning killer; she is a person who works for a higher good, longs for love, and seeks atonement. Zoe's performance was incredibly emotional, especially when it came to her interactions with other Guardians like Drax (Dave Bautista), Rocket (Bradley Cooper), and Peter Quill (Chris Pratt). Gamora was given even more dimension by the emotional depth of her relationships, particularly her bond with Quill, which elevated her beyond simply being a fierce warrior.

Both Neytiri and Gamora are legendary because they defy the expectations of conventional female action heroes. They are fully formed characters with their storylines, goals, and personal development—not just romantic interests or sidekicks. In a field where male heroes and protagonists frequently dominate, Zoe's portrayal of these powerful women with emotional sensitivity and power sets them apart. For fans worldwide, Neytiri and Gamora came to represent grit, self-reliance, and tenacity, and Zoe's performances gave them life in ways that left an enduring impression.

Zoe underwent extensive physical training as part of her commitment to these roles. She trained in martial arts and sword combat to depict Neytiri as a proficient warrior in **Avatar**. Neytiri's battle sequences are among the most memorable in the movie because of Zoe's dedication to the training and the role's physicality, which is essential to the character's personality. Similarly, Zoe put a lot of effort into improving her fighting abilities and physical condition for **Guardians of the Galaxy** to make Gamora's battle scenes as realistic and robust as possible. Her rigorous physical training demonstrated that these parts required more than simply acting; they needed her to mentally and physically inhabit the characters.

Furthermore, regarding the technology utilized to give the figures life, Zoe's work in these two roles was revolutionary. To transfer Zoe's performance into the Na'vi persona and maintain her distinct acting style even in the CGI-heavy environment of Pandora, **Avatar** primarily relied on motion capture technology. Despite playing Gamora in a live-action film for **Guardians of the Galaxy**, Zoe used state-of-the-art visual effects to make her look more powerful and otherworldly. These movies demonstrated Zoe's ability to use cutting-edge tools and filmmaking methods without sacrificing the integrity of her characters.

In addition to portraying challenging roles, Zoe's portrayals of Neytiri and Gamora aimed to represent nuanced women with depth, strength, and sensitivity. Thanks to her roles, she broke down barriers in Hollywood and established herself as an inspiration to people of all ages. She demonstrated how multifaceted, emotionally complex, and fierce human women might be in movies. With Neytiri and Gamora, Zoe cemented her status as one of Hollywood's most gifted and significant actresses, able to play strong characters that would impact future generations.

Chapter 5: More Than Just a Star

Zoe Saldana is a complex person whose life encompasses much more than her acting career. Her life behind the scenes, her commitment to her family, and her job as a mother have profoundly influenced her identity, even if her stunning on-screen performances have drawn attention from audiences worldwide. Zoe has demonstrated that she is just as committed to her family as her work by successfully juggling her demanding career with her love for them.

Behind the scenes, Zoe's career has been influenced by her motivation and the encouragement of her loved ones. Even though a large portion of her job is publicly visible, Zoe has been careful to keep her private life private and grounded. She is cautious about what she discloses and frequently emphasizes the importance of keeping her family life secret. She attributes her ability to maintain composure and concentration in the hectic entertainment world to her strong familial values. Growing up in a multicultural family that valued loyalty and love, Zoe realized early on the value of preserving deep connections and remaining true to her heritage. She upholds this ideal in her adult life and with her family.

Zoe frequently talks about how her success is fueled by her family, who are fundamental to who she is. She has stated that her mother served as her role model, raising Zoe and her brothers in the United States with love, hard work, and discipline. Zoe has instilled this tradition of love and strength in her children. Zoe has always been honest about how important it is to provide for her family, and she frequently expresses her gratitude for her mother's continued wisdom and guidance.

Being a mother is one of Zoe's most essential tasks in life. She wed actor Marco Perego in 2014, and the two had three sons. Speaking openly about the pleasures and difficulties of parenting, Zoe has highlighted how it has significantly altered her perspective on life. She now understands love more deeply and has a new sense of purpose due to becoming a mother. According to Zoe, motherhood has been a life-changing experience that taught her to be patient, humble, and value each moment. Zoe has always put her responsibilities as a mother first, juggling the challenges of raising a family with her professional commitments despite her well-known career.

As her mother taught her, she also advocates for instilling empathy, respect, and hard work in her kids. Zoe has frequently expressed her desire for her kids to grow up with a strong sense of ethnic pride, an open mind to diverse viewpoints, and self-assurance in their identities. She feels that to help her kids become well-rounded people who comprehend and value the world around them, it is crucial to expose them to a variety of cultures, languages, and experiences. Her devotion to supporting her kids' development reflects her pursuit of greatness in her acting career.

Beyond her immediate family, Zoe is dedicated to her family. She has a close-knit family and has always stressed the value of building a loving and supportive community. She frequently celebrates holidays and life milestones with her extended family. Zoe places a high value on this support system since it keeps her centered in her hectic work schedule. She has also been known to provide her coworkers and fellow actors the same warmth and concern, frequently developing enduring connections on set that go beyond work. One of the reasons she is so well-liked in her personal and Hollywood lives is her capacity to build close relationships.

Zoe has consistently upheld her essential beliefs of family, love, and balance despite the demands of her career in Hollywood. She is committed to being a hands-on mother, taking breaks from her work to spend time with her kids and observe their development. Zoe has learned to establish limits and put her priorities first as a working mother in a field that frequently requires long hours and demanding schedules. She has made it clear how much she cherishes her time at home with her family, but she has also been candid about the difficulties she faces in striking a work-life balance, particularly when traveling for movie shoots.

In addition to her commitment to her wife and kids, Zoe has strongly supported women in the entertainment sector. She often discusses the value of gender equality and representation in Hollywood. She is devoted to giving her kids a better future and ensuring they are raised in a society where women and people of color have equal rights and a voice in the arts. Her experiences as a woman of color in the entertainment sector, where she has witnessed firsthand the obstacles women encounter in obtaining opportunities, equitable pay, and representation, are the foundation of this advocacy. Zoe uses her position to encourage positive change and young women to pursue their goals in the same way she did.

Zoe's attitude toward parenting and home life demonstrates her capacity to balance her professional and personal ideals. She feels that the two are not incompatible and that her motherhood does not have to suffer because of her career in Hollywood. Her family is her compass, and she strives to maintain those bonds while pursuing her interests and goals. Zoe is a living example of how one may succeed professionally yet be devoted to the people they love and care for. In addition to being a role model in the profession, she is also adored by her fans and those who know her personally because of her dedication to family, being a hands-on mother, and keeping perspective and balance.

Chapter 6: Strong Women in Movies

In addition to her extraordinary acting ability, Zoe Saldana's career in Hollywood is based on the muscular, complex women she has represented. From **Avatar's** feisty Neytiri to **Guardians of the Galaxy's** resolute Gamora, Zoe has emerged as an advocate for strong female characters in movies—characters who encourage girls everywhere to embrace their courage, power, and brilliance. By demonstrating to young girls that they can be leaders, fighters, and thinkers in their own lives, Zoe provides entertainment and conveys a powerful message about self-worth and empowerment.

Although physical prowess and fighting prowess are undoubtedly essential parts of the characters Zoe portrays, they are not the only characteristics that characterize them. Their mental toughness, bravery in the face of difficulty, and cunning in handling challenging circumstances make these characters stand out. By making these qualities personal and approachable, Zoe teaches girls that strength can take various forms.

Zoe's portrayal of Neytiri, a bold and brave Na'vi warrior, in **Avatar** highlights the significance of standing up for your beliefs and defending the environment. In addition to being a talented combatant, Neytiri has a strong bond with tradition, wisdom, and the natural world. Even amid extreme adversity, Zoe provides Neytiri with an inner strength that comes through. Neytiri's ability to strike a balance between compassion and strength is what makes her so inspirational. She demonstrates to young girls that being strong and fierce while having empathy and concern for others is possible. Girls worldwide can learn from her steadfast resolve and faith in her culture how powerful it is to hold on to your convictions in the face of opposition.

Similarly, Zoe's portrayal of Gamora, the "most dangerous woman in the universe," in **Guardians of the**

Galaxy highlights fortitude, self-redemption, and leadership. Gamora had a problematic past because she was raised by the vicious Thanos and received assassination training. Gamora, however, refuses to let her traumatic past dictate her destiny. Gamora is given depth and humanity by Zoe, who demonstrates that despite one's past transgressions, one can still decide to strive for justice, a better life, and personal atonement. Through Gamora, Zoe shows girls that strength is more than just physical ability; it's also about having the guts to adapt, mature, and make the correct choices despite adversity. Girls are inspired to embrace their leadership potential and have the courage to make difficult decisions by Gamora, a figure who knows how to take command in trying circumstances.

Zoe's ability to represent both of these characters with such realism also conveys a strong message about the importance of intelligence. In addition to their physical strength, Neytiri and Gamora are intelligent, cunning, and quick-witted. Neytiri protects Pandora and her loved ones by using her knowledge of the land, the natural world, and her people; as much of her power as her combat prowess comes from her wisdom. Gamora's intelligence is demonstrated in **Guardians of the Galaxy** by how she outwits her adversaries, makes strategic choices, and maneuvers through difficult circumstances. Young girls learn from these roles that strength isn't just about having muscles; it's also about utilizing your heart, head, and intuition to make the correct decisions and defend your morals.

In addition to these individual traits, Zoe demonstrates the value of sisterhood and teamwork. Neytiri and Gamora are both strong women in their own right, but they also collaborate with others—especially other women—to accomplish their objectives. Gamora and the other Guardians in Guardians of the Galaxy have a strong bond, and her relationship with the crew exemplifies the value of cooperation, mutual trust, and support. The lesson is unmistakable: We are all stronger when we support one another; nobody can succeed alone.

Furthermore, Zoe's commitment to portraying powerful women goes beyond her on-screen personas. Being a Latina woman in Hollywood, Zoe has taken advantage of her position to dispel the myths surrounding women of color in movies. She has discussed the value of representation and her desire to encourage young girls—particularly those from marginalized communities—to think they can be heroes, too. Zoe has stated that she views herself as an example for young girls who might not see many personalities like themselves on the big screen. Her desire to empower, see, and hear girls worldwide is further supported by her support of improved representation of women in Hollywood, especially women of color.

Her impact extends beyond the roles she portrays and includes her behavior. Off-screen, Zoe is well-known for her dedication to women's rights and her enthusiasm for promoting gender equality-related causes. She frequently speaks out on topics including the value of mental health, work-life balance, and women's empowerment. She is a strong role model for females who look up to her not only for her acting but also for her character and her desire to stand up for what is right since her support of these causes reflects the bravery and fortitude she exhibits in her performances.

Zoe Saldana's legendary roles in movies like **Avatar** and **Guardians of the Galaxy** have made her a symbol of bravery, strength, and brilliance for females worldwide. She demonstrates to them that one can be strong, independent, and fierce without compromising one's compassion, empathy, or openness. Young girls learn from Zoe's characters that it's acceptable to be complex, accept imperfections, and discover power in your voice. Zoe gives a more varied and inspiring representation of what it is to be a woman by portraying both intense and emotionally complex characters, challenging the limited representation of women in movies.

Chapter 7: A Heart for Change

In addition to being a trailblazing actor, Zoe Saldana is an ardent supporter of numerous humanitarian causes. She has continuously used her position to advocate for causes that are important to her, such as mental health awareness, environmental preservation, and racial and gender equality. Zoe strongly believes in leveraging her notoriety and power to raise awareness of important issues that impact people globally and give voice to underrepresented groups. Her commitment to social concerns reflects her sincere desire to improve the world through her on-screen personas and real, significant action.

For Zoe, racial and gender equality are among the most important reasons. Zoe has witnessed the difficulties of being underrepresented and frequently typecast in clichéd parts as a woman of color in Hollywood. She has advocated for diversity in the entertainment sector and the significance of media representation for young people, particularly those from marginalized areas. From acting to directing to producing, Zoe is a vocal supporter of expanding possibilities for women of color in the entertainment industry. She puts a lot of effort into developing and promoting initiatives representing our diverse society because she understands how important representation is.

Additionally, Zoe has advocated for the more significant battle for gender equality by using her voice. She is vocal about the value of women standing by each other and the necessity of elevating female voices in areas where they have historically been underrepresented. Zoe consistently uses her position to advocate for gender equity, whether it's by calling for equal pay or inspiring young women to seek jobs in industries that men have historically controlled. She is very outspoken about the necessity for women to take charge of their own stories, both in real life and on screen. Many young women who want to change their communities and careers now look up to Zoe because of her public support of numerous women's empowerment programs.

Environmental conservation is another concern close to Zoe's heart. Zoe has continuously supported efforts to save our planet in a world of climate change and ecological degradation. She supports several environmental groups that fight deforestation, conserve natural resources, and save endangered species. Her dedication to environmental problems is further supported by her portrayal of Neytiri in **Avatar**, a heroine with a strong connection to nature. Zoe has frequently discussed her love of nature and her desire to instill in her kids a respect for the environment in interviews. She stresses the significance of teaching the next generation how to be good environmental stewards and safeguard the planet. In Zoe's opinion, prioritizing sustainability, cutting waste, and making thoughtful decisions that benefit the environment for coming generations are some of the most important things we can do as a society and as people.

Another area in which Zoe has had a significant influence is her commitment to raising awareness of mental health issues. She has been candid about her battles with mental health and the need to eradicate the stigma associated with mental illness. As a public figure, Zoe has been open about her challenges and how she has learned to manage the highs and lows of being in the spotlight. Zoe wants to inspire others to prioritize their mental health and get treatment by sharing her own experiences. To promote a broader discussion about the significance of mental health care in today's society, she has backed several programs and projects that center on mental health advocacy.

Beyond these fields, Zoe firmly commits to topics about children's rights, education, and the empowerment of underrepresented groups. Because she thinks having access to high-quality education is essential to ending the cycle of poverty, she supports groups that strive to give underprivileged kids educational opportunities. Because she understands the hardships encountered by those compelled to flee their countries because of conflict or violence, Zoe has also been an outspoken supporter of immigrants and refugees. She uses her position to spread the word about the value of helping people in need and collaborates closely with groups that support and advocate for displaced communities.

Speaking up is only one aspect of Zoe's dedication to these topics; she also actively participates in charitable endeavors and practical initiatives to truly change things. She frequently participates in fundraising activities, donates her time to help with different projects, and offers her voice to causes that share her beliefs. Zoe is a steadfast and continuous supporter of change, whether by raising awareness of climate change, fighting for women's rights, or inspiring young people to follow their passions.

Zoe's ability to reconcile her convictions with her public presence makes her unique. Even if it may not be the simplest or most popular course of action, she has never shied away from using her celebrity to raise awareness of the topics she believes in. The foundation of Zoe's strategy is authenticity; she talks from the heart and works to bring about change in a significant and long-lasting way. She encourages her followers to take action in their own lives, supports other activists, and elevates the voices of marginalized communities via her platform.

Zoe's influence on social concerns reflects her strong personal convictions and faith in the transformative potential of change. She continues to motivate people to fight for justice and equality, to become champions for the causes they care about, and to strive for a more compassionate world by using her voice for good. By doing this, Zoe demonstrates that celebrity can be used for good and that everyone can change the world by standing up for what's right, regardless of background.

Chapter 8: Learning from Challenges

There have been obstacles in Zoe Saldana's path to Hollywood fame. Zoe has experienced challenging times that have put her grit and resiliency to the test, both personally and professionally. But instead of allowing these difficulties to define her, she has seized the chance to develop, gain knowledge, and eventually become the woman she is today. Because of her capacity to endure hardship and become stronger, she inspires many, particularly young people who might encounter challenges.

Growing up in a multicultural home with a tight budget was one of Zoe's first difficulties. Zoe was born in New Jersey to a Puerto Rican mother and a Dominican father. She spent much of her early years in the Dominican Republic before returning to the United States when she was ten. Zoe frequently talks about how her parents struggled financially and how hard they fought to support their family. She learned the importance of tenacity and diligence from her mother's efforts, particularly as a single mom. These early difficulties formed her perspective on life, which taught her never to take anything for granted. Despite the challenges, Zoe always remained hopeful and determined and found strength in her family and cultural roots.

Zoe also had to deal with the difficulties of being a Latina in Hollywood, where parts for persons of color were frequently restricted and stereotyped, as a young lady breaking into the competitive acting field. Zoe struggled to find situations that would allow her to show off her entire range as an actress in her early career, and she was often put in one-dimensional or supporting roles. She frequently felt frustrated by the lack of representation in the field, but Zoe refused to let the setback stop her from moving forward and fighting for better possibilities. She was committed to demonstrating that women of color could perform dynamic, nuanced parts free from stereotypes.

She encountered innumerable rejections while pursuing these chances, but she persisted. She learned critical lessons about perseverance and resilience from each setback. Her efforts eventually paid off as she began to secure more prominent roles like those in **Avatar** and **Guardians of the Galaxy**, where she could show off her skills and establish a new precedent for women of color in major, action-packed roles. Zoe's achievement is evidence of her perseverance and defiance of the constraints others attempted to impose on her.

Zoe had another difficult time in her early years as a mother. She has been candid about the challenges she had juggling her personal and professional lives, especially following the birth of her first child. Zoe battled guilt and the ongoing pressure to strike the ideal balance between her busy career and her desire to be a hands-on, present mother, just like many working women do. Her first time as a mother was difficult, and she frequently felt conflicted between her mom and actress roles. But Zoe had to redefine balance for herself to overcome this obstacle. After realizing that "perfect balance" did not exist, she concentrated on being present when it was most important. Due to this event, Zoe learned to put her health first and realized that it's acceptable to seek assistance when necessary.

Personally, Zoe has also had to deal with the devastating loss of her father, who was a significant part of her life. Zoe suffered a severe emotional scar when her father died when she was just nine years old. Zoe frequently looked to her mother for direction as a child without her father. Although this loss influenced Zoe's early life, it motivated her to become a muscular, self-reliant adult. Zoe has talked about how she has strived to be the kind of mother and partner her father would be proud of and how this tragedy has taught her the value of remembering the time we spend with our loved ones. Her perspective on life has also changed as a result of her father's passing; she is now reminded to cherish the time she spends with her family and to live in the now.

The public has also criticized Zoe during her career, mainly how she portrayed well-known figures like Gamora and Neytiri. As a woman of color performing major parts, she frequently received acclaim and criticism, with some viewers wondering why she was chosen for these prominent parts. Zoe's portrayal of Neytiri in **Avatar** drew criticism, with some critics raising concerns about whether a Latina actress should play a character of a different ethnicity. Her performance as Gamora elicited conflicting responses from critics, some more interested in her looks than her acting. But Zoe has always handled these difficulties with poise and hasn't allowed criticism to derail her from her objectives. She is confident that artists should be allowed to play various complicated characters, regardless of their color or background. In addition to staying unapologetic, Zoe has continuously taken criticism as a chance to grow and evaluate.

Zoe has persevered and stayed committed to her objectives despite these obstacles. She now understands that being strong means confronting hardship and growing from it rather than running away. Her ability to adjust, develop, and flourish in adversity characterizes her success. She has grown as a person and an artist due to every hardship, whether it be a personal loss, difficulties in her career, or the demands of being a working mother.

Chapter 9: The Power of Being Yourself

Zoe Saldana's success in Hollywood results from her steadfast dedication to remaining true to herself as much as her talent and tenacity. Zoe has consistently prioritized authenticity above popularity in a field that frequently requires conformity and pressures actors to fit a specific model. One of the main reasons for her success has been her dedication to being herself, which still inspires people everywhere. We may learn from Zoe's tale that the strength of being yourself is found in having the guts to embrace your individuality and pursue your passions despite any challenges.

She had a clear idea of her identity and goals from an early age. Her Puerto Rican and Dominican ancestry significantly impacted her upbringing in a multicultural home. Zoe has frequently discussed how her upbringing influenced who she is and made her feel proud of her roots. She valued the parts of herself that made her unique and accepted her culture rather than attempting to fit into a specific box or follow trends. Her self-assurance and pride in who she is have served as a constant source of motivation throughout her acting career, allowing her to play various challenging roles.

Zoe has always defied expectations in a field where actors are frequently urged to portray roles that adhere to a particular plot or aesthetic. Zoe has consistently pursued jobs that question the existing quo and enable her to demonstrate her entire range as an actress, from her well-known parts in **Avatar** and **Guardians of the Galaxy** to her more recent work. By doing this, she has demonstrated that being true to yourself involves more than just saying "no" to things that don't fit your beliefs; it also entails actively looking for chances to develop, change, and reveal your true self to the world. Rather than choosing what may be viewed as the "safe" or "popular" option, Zoe has continuously selected roles that represent her unique interests, values, and passions. Her genuineness has made her stand out in a field where many performers constantly change who they are to stay contemporary.

Beyond the screen, Zoe has decided to play parts that align with her principles. Her views on the value of diversity and representation in Hollywood have been openly expressed. The idea that everyone should be able to see themselves represented in fiction, regardless of gender, ethnicity, or origin, is the foundation of Zoe's work with characters like Neytiri and Gamora. By assuming these roles, Zoe has challenged the long-standing preconceptions about women and people of color in Hollywood by using her platform. She has established herself as a role model not just because of her roles but also because of her decisions and how she upholds her morals in the face of social pressure.

Choosing the less-traveled path has also allowed her to remain loyal to herself. Zoe has decided to follow her passion and work on projects that speak to her more deeply, even though she could have readily accepted more popular parts or brought more financial success.

She has played parts that fit her passions for action, fantasy, and science fiction—genres that let her work with strong, multifaceted characters. According to Zoe, her love of storytelling and her ambition to create strong, resilient, and complex characters are the main reasons she is passionate about these genres. By pursuing her passion, Zoe has become successful and produced a body of work she is proud of, solidifying her status as one of Hollywood's most respected and versatile actors.

She demonstrates the value of authenticity in her personal life by juggling her work and responsibilities as a wife and mother. In interviews, she discussed the significance of maintaining her sense of reality and prioritizing the most important things to her. Zoe has consistently stated that her family comes first, even though her career is highly essential. She has been candid about how she tries to keep a healthy work-life balance and the difficulties she faces in juggling the obligations of being a working mother with her desire to be there for her kids. By doing this, Zoe demonstrates that being authentic includes accepting all aspects of your life, not just the glitzy or publicly apparent ones. She demonstrates that it's possible to lead a happy and genuine life, even in the spotlight, by upholding her morals and putting her family first.

Zoe's dedication to authenticity is a potent reminder that success is not determined by approval from others or outside validation. In a society that frequently places a premium on status or fitting in, Zoe's story shows us that true success comes from pursuing our goals regardless of what others may believe or anticipate. She illustrates how we are more likely to find happiness and attain a more profound degree of success—one that is personally meaningful and fulfilling—when we persist in pursuing our goals and value our individuality.

We learn the value of tenacity from Zoe's narrative as well. The journey will always be challenging if you stay loyal to yourself. The important thing is to keep moving forward and remain focused on your objectives despite obstacles, rejections, and setbacks along the path. Throughout her career, Zoe has encountered several challenges, ranging from early difficulties landing fulfilling parts to handling criticism from the public. She has, however, stayed true to her devotion to genuineness throughout it all. She has never let these obstacles stop her from pursuing her goals or compromising her morals. Instead, she has embraced these failures as chances to grow, learn, and remain faithful to her mission.

Chapter 10: Family and Friendship

Zoe Saldana's success in Hollywood is mainly due to the solid foundation of love, support, and loyalty she receives from her family and close friends rather than just her skill or diligence. Zoe has often underlined the value of her relationships with those closest to her, and it is evident that her family and friends have played a crucial role in supporting her as she navigates the difficulties of her personal and professional lives.

Her foundation has always been her family. Zoe was raised by a single mother when her father passed away when she was only nine years old, and she has often talked about how her mother was crucial in forming her morals and character. Zoe persevered through challenging circumstances because of her mother's grit, tenacity, and commitment to their family. Zoe learned the value of endurance, hard work, and sacrifice from her mother, who worked nonstop to provide for her children when she was growing up. Zoe and her mother are still quite close, and the actress has always found strength in their relationship.

Another significant component of Zoe's support network has been her siblings. Zoe has a special bond with her sisters, who have supported her through the highs and lows of her career. Her family has always supported her in pursuing her goals while remaining rooted in reality. Zoe feels incredibly secure because of her family's love and support, which is particularly helpful in a notorious field for its unpredictability and ongoing pressure. Zoe frequently talks about how her family reminds her of the value of remaining modest, kind, and rooted in her heritage, which helps her maintain perspective on what matters in life.

Zoe's network of friends expanded along with her job; many have become like family. Over the years, Zoe has formed strong bonds with her co-stars, including other actresses like Jennifer Lopez, who has been Zoe's friend and mentor for a long time. These friendships are based on respect for one another, sincere personal ties, and everyday experiences on set. Zoe has frequently discussed the value of surrounding herself with positive, encouraging people in her personal and professional life. During the most trying times, her friends provide solace, counsel, and laughter, and their encouragement keeps her goal-focused.

Additionally, Zoe's close-knit circle of friends has been a tremendous source of emotional support, especially throughout the most trying times in her life. Zoe knows that she can always count on her friends to provide sympathetic ear and sage advice, whether juggling the demands of a celebrity or juggling parenthood and a profession. Many of Zoe's closest relationships are with people aware of the pressures of the entertainment business and offer her a haven to be herself without worrying about what other people think of her public persona.

The assistance Zoe receives from her husband, Marco Perego, whom she married in 2013, is another critical component of her family and social network. Zoe and Marco prioritize their family and each other's happiness, and their relationship has been one of mutual respect and affection. Zoe has said how happy she is to have Marco at her side. Marco is an artist renowned for being private and encouraging of Zoe's career. By juggling their separate jobs with the joint duty of raising their three children, they have created a loving and understanding family. Because of Marco's steadfast support, Zoe can give her all to her career without compromising her family life, which she much appreciates.

She is firmly committed to her extended family and close friends. She takes pride in maintaining ties to her cultural heritage and has always stayed close to her roots in Puerto Rico and the Dominican Republic. Throughout her career, she has received love and support from her extended family, which includes aunts, uncles, and cousins. They also often celebrate her accomplishments and milestones. No matter how high her career rises,

Zoe's relationship with her extended family keeps her grounded by reminding her of her modest beginnings.

Zoe's approach to work selections is also greatly influenced by her ties with her family and friends. She appreciates their counsel and frequently consults them before making significant career decisions. Even though she has a group of agents and advisors, Zoe has always stressed the value of speaking with those closest to her—those who know her best and care for her well. In addition to being the first to congratulate her on her accomplishments, her family and friends are also there to provide candid criticism when necessary, assisting her in making choices consistent with her values and long-term objectives.

It should come as no surprise that Zoe feels strongly about the value of preserving solid, sustaining connections. She knows how simple it is to lose touch with what matters in a field as high-pressure and cutthroat as Hollywood. She knows that her close relationships with family and friends give her the emotional support, motivation, and perspective she needs to achieve, which is why she highly values them. For Zoe, success is about the people who support you, push you, and share in your most treasured moments rather than merely achievements or honors.

Fun facts about Zoe Saldana

Zoe is proud of her ethnic background. She was born in New Jersey to a Puerto Rican mother and a Dominican father. Before returning to the United States, she lived in the Dominican Republic for most of her early years.

2. A Love for Dance
Zoe was a gifted dancer before she became an actress. She attended the esteemed ECOS Espacio de Danza Academy in the Dominican Republic to study ballet, jazz, and modern dance.

3. Breakout Role
Zoe's breakthrough performance was as an ardent ballet dancer in the 2000 movie Center Stage. This performance demonstrated her dancing prowess and aided in her Hollywood recognition.

4. Science Fiction Queen

Zoe is renowned for portraying strong, recognizable roles in well-known science fiction series. She became famous in the genre after playing Neytiri in **Avatar** (2009) and Gamora in **Guardians of the Galaxy** (2014).

5. Vocal About Representation:
Zoe strongly believes Hollywood needs more representation. She frequently speaks out on the subject because she thinks actors from various backgrounds must have their stories told on television.

6. Mother of Three:
Zoe and her husband, Marco Perego, are parents to three boys. Although she keeps her family life very quiet, she has stated that one of her favorite things is being a mother.

7. A Star in **Avatar** Sequel:
Zoe continues her legacy in the ground-breaking film series by reprising her role as Neytiri in the much-awaited **Avatar** sequel (**Avatar: The Way of Water**).

8. Speaks Spanish Fluently

Zoe was raised in the Dominican Republic and is fluent in Spanish. She also supports the inclusion of more Latinx performers in the entertainment sector.

9. Fashion Icon:

Zoe's exquisite style is well-known. She is frequently commended for her stylish and sophisticated appearance, whether on the red carpet or in casual settings.

10. Green and Blue:

Zoe has demonstrated her versatility and dedication to her jobs by playing the blue-skinned Neytiri and the green-skinned Gamora beneath a lot of makeup.

These fascinating details shed light on Zoe's distinct upbringing, interests, and achievements on and off screen.

Conclusion: Reaching for your stars

No matter the size of their dreams, everyone has them. While some visions are loud and audacious, others are whispers. The narrative of Zoe Saldana serves as a potent reminder that if you put in the necessary effort, remain loyal to yourself, and have faith in your capacity to change the world, no dream is too huge to pursue or a goal too difficult to accomplish.

At the beginning of Zoe's journey, there was no obvious route to fame and wealth. As with many of our adventures, it was indeed filled with doubts, hard effort, and uncertainties. Zoe stands out, though, because she never gave up. She recognized that success is frequently a rocky road and that perseverance is crucial, especially when things don't seem to be going your way. Even when success appeared far off, she had faith in herself and continued to strive toward her goals every day.

For young readers, Zoe's story reminds them that no matter what obstacles you face, it's worthwhile to pursue your dreams. Regardless of your career goals—acting, science, art, or something else—it's critical to start someplace, take the initial step, and never lose hope in your abilities. There will always be challenges, whether it's self-doubt, fear of failing, or other people's opinions. The important thing is to keep moving forward with confidence and commitment. You can overcome obstacles and demonstrate that your goals are worthwhile, just like Zoe did.

We may learn from Zoe's journey that it's acceptable to encounter obstacles along the way. Sometimes, the most valuable lessons we can learn from those setbacks help us succeed even more in the future. Despite several "no"s, setbacks, and rejections, Zoe knew, adjusted, and discovered new ways to improve every time. Failure is a part of the process that makes you stronger and more intelligent; it's not the end. Continue to learn from those experiences, maintain your curiosity, and never give up because every attempt brings you one step closer to realizing your goals.

Zoe's life also teaches us the importance of being authentic. It's simple to be sucked into trying to be like someone else or fit in, but real success comes from embracing your individuality. Be proud of your identity, background, and beliefs, just as Zoe did. The world needs your voice, your thoughts, and your skills. Your ability to change the world will increase as you remain loyal to who you are. It would help to take pride that no one else is like you.

Remember to show kindness and encouragement to everyone around you as you pursue your goals. Relationships with mentors, family, and friends may have a profound impact, as Zoe's experience demonstrates. These individuals support you when you need it, encourage you when you succeed, and provide guidance when you're unsure what to do next. As Zoe does with her family and friends, surround yourself with people who support you and inspire you to keep working for your objectives.

Lastly, remember that you are in charge of your path. You can decide how far you want to go and what direction your ambitions will take. You can influence your course and leave your mark on the world, just like Zoe did. If you have passion, tenacity, and self-belief, you can accomplish everything you want, even if it takes time and work.

Therefore, feel free to aim for your stars as you travel through life. Be bold, have huge dreams, and remember the endless possibilities. Like Zoe, you can realize the many options ahead of you. Never lose hope, never give up, and forget that you may achieve greatness in your unique manner.